The Good Book

by

Matthew, Mark, Luke and John
as told to

David Evans

drawings by Sherman

PRICE / STERN / SLOAN
Publishers, Inc., Los Angeles

Fifth Printing — July 1973

Copyright © 1970, 1972 by David Evans
Published by Price/Stern/Sloan Publishers, Inc.
410 North La Cienega Blvd., Los Angeles, California 90048
Printed in the United States of America. All rights reserved.
Library of Congress Catalog Card Number: 73-186697
ISBN: 0-8431-0129-6

the Three Wise Men

"Cute little devil."

"He has your nose and chin, Mary, but he has God's eyes."

Joseph and Mary

"I'd like you to meet my wife, the Virgin Mary."

"Look, Joseph! Jesus took his first step!"

"Eat all your vegetables or you won't grow up to be a big strong Messiah."

the Years in the Carpenter Shop

"Hey, wait a minute. I just came in here for a little wood work, not a <u>sermon!</u>"

the Ministry begins

JESUS CHRIST CARPENTER SHOP

FOR SALE
OWNER ENTERING
NEW LINE
OF WORK

"Unaccustomed as I am to public speaking . . ."

Christ's old gang wonders about him

"Have you noticed how **different** Jesus is acting since he became the Saviour?"

Christ journeys to Cana

"Judging from your halo, I'd say you're a stranger in these parts, Mister."

Christ heals the sick

"Normally I don't make house calls . . ."

Christ and his disciples

"I have a message for you men from God this morning."

Christ preaches to the multitudes

"Is there anyone in the audience today from Galilee?"

the Disciples seek new converts

"When do we get to add some girl disciples?"

Christ heals the blind man

"You'll never guess what happened to me downtown today."

The Disciples

"I'm getting a little tired of Jesus's holier-than-thou attitude."

"Such a nice young man. I wonder if he's married?"

"There's a guy outside sounding off about your miracles.
Shall I turn the other cheek, or can I belt him?"

"I'm afraid Lazarus is dead, madame. Only a miracle
could help him now."

the Virgin Mary

"My boy Jesus has plenty of time to heal lepers, raise people from the dead and walk on the water, but do you think he has time to write his mother?"

word of Christ's ministry spreads

"Surely not <u>the</u> Jesus Christ!"

"Judas, if anything should ever happen to me, could you take over?"

the Miracle of the Loaves and the Fishes

"He forgot the tartar sauce."

Mary Magdalene visits a fortune teller

"I see a man entering your life soon. He is tall, dark and handsome and has a halo."

"Some miracle! It's been three weeks since the Sermon on the Mount and we're still eating left-overs."

"You know, Matthew, all of this sure would make one hell of a book!"

the Virgin Mary grants an interview to a scribe

" . . . But aside from performing miracles, was Jesus in any way an unusual child?"

"Jesus, do you ever have days when you just figure
'The hell with it!'?"

"Did you ever notice that, whenever there's a lot of work to be done, you-know-who has to go pray?"

the Last Supper

"I think it's fun to eat out."

Christ before Pontius Pilate

"They tell me you're a real weird-o, Jesus."

"Now when the guard comes in with the food, I'll grab his keys and you jump him from behind."

"You again!"

Judas's mother laments

"Judas wasn't a bad boy really. He just fell in with the wrong crowd."

Matthew begins the Scriptures

"I can either name them the <u>Old Testament</u> and the <u>New Testament</u> or I could call them <u>God</u> and <u>Son of God</u>."

Christ joins God in heaven

"Son, someday this will all be yours."

This book is published by

PRICE / STERN / SLOAN

Publishers, Inc.

whose other splendid titles include such literary classics as:

YOU WERE BORN ON A ROTTEN DAY
FIRST WIFE, SECOND WIFE
HOW TO BE A JEWISH MOTHER
HOW TO BE AN ITALIAN
SHELLEY BERMAN'S CLEANS & DIRTYS
LOVE IS WHEN YOU MEET A MAN WHO
DOESN'T LIVE WITH HIS MOTHER
HOW TO TELL IF YOUR HUSBAND IS CHEATING ON YOU
THE POWER OF POSITIVE PESSIMISM
THE WORLD'S WORST JOKES
THE VERY IMPORTANT PERSON NOTEBOOK

and many, many more

If not available at your bookseller's they may
be ordered directly from the publisher. For complete list write:

Dept. GB-5

PRICE / STERN / SLOAN

Publishers, Inc., Los Angeles

**410 North La Cienega Boulevard
Los Angeles, California 90048**

PUBLISHED BY

PRICE
STERN
SLOAN